THINK CHESS- WIN BUSINESS

Jerremy Specter-Mendam

Table of Contents

Chapter 8: Advanced Strategies in Chess and Business

- Beyond Basics: Mastering Complex Tactics

- Leveraging Weaknesses and Strategic Sacrifices

- Positional Play, Pinning, Forking, and Other Advanced Techniques

Conclusion: Beyond the Board - Strategic Mastery in Business

- Synthesis of Chess Principles for Business Success

- The Continuous Journey of Learning and Adaptation

Appendices

- Glossary of Chess and Business Terms

- Case Studies of Chess Strategies in Business

- Recommended Resources for Further Learning

In this book, we delve into the fascinating world where the ancient game of chess serves as a metaphor for the strategic and tactical battles waged in the business arena. Both chess and business require a blend of strategic foresight, critical decision-making, and the agility to adapt to ever-changing scenarios. This book explores the profound parallels between maneuvering pieces on a chessboard and steering a company towards success in the competitive marketplace. Through a series of insightful chapters, readers will learn how the principles that guide chess masters can also inform and inspire business leaders to make smarter decisions, anticipate competitors' moves, and achieve their strategic objectives. Join us on this captivating journey to discover how the timeless game of chess can illuminate the path to business mastery.

The game of chess.

Chess is a game with a rich history that spans over 1500 years, with its origins often traced back to India, around the 6th century AD. Originating from earlier versions of forms of the game, one of the earliest was called "Chaturanga," was much like the chess we know today but was played on an 8x8 grid board with pieces that closely resemble modern chess pieces, each with its own set of movements. Chaturanga is considered a precursor to several strategic board games that evolved in different parts of the world.

Over the years, the game made its way to Persia, where it became known as "Shatranj." The Persians introduced two significant changes or variants: the names of some pieces and the starting phrase "Shah Mat" (the King is helpless), from which the term "checkmate" derives. When the Islamic conquest of Persia took place, chess spread across the Islamic caliphates, reaching parts of Europe through both the Iberian Peninsula and the Byzantine Empire.

By the 15th century, chess had undergone significant evolution in Europe, leading to changes in the movement of several pieces, which accelerated the game. This modern version of chess, often referred to as "Queen's Chess," increased the power of the queen, making it the most dominant piece on the board. These modifications marked the transition to the game of chess as it is recognized today.

The 19th century was a turning point for chess, moving it from a leisurely pastime to a highly competitive sport. The first official chess tournament was held in London in 1851. This period also saw the standardization of rules and the establishment of chess clubs and organizations around the world. The International Chess Federation (FIDE) was founded in 1924, further solidifying the game's global appeal and competitive structure.

The study of chess has produced an extensive body of literature, ranging from opening theory to endgame studies. The 20th century introduced another dimension to chess through computers. In 1997, IBM's Deep Blue defeated reigning World Champion Garry Kasparov in a historic match, marking the first time a reigning world champion lost to a computer under standard chess tournament conditions. This event highlighted the advancements in artificial intelligence and computer science.

Today, chess remains a popular global sport, enjoyed by millions of amateurs and professionals. The internet has transformed how people learn, play, and watch chess, with online platforms and streaming services making the game more accessible than ever. The 2020 Netflix series "The Queen's Gambit" sparked a renewed interest in chess, leading to a surge in online play.

Chess's enduring appeal lies in its blend of art, science, and competition. Its rich history and deep strategic complexity continue to captivate and challenge players around the world, making it a timeless game that spans cultures and generations.

The game of business.

The history of business is a broad and complex narrative that spans thousands of years, evolving from simple barter systems to the complex global economy we see today. Here's a condensed overview of some key milestones in the development of business practices and economic systems throughout history.

Early Beginnings: The roots of business can be traced back to ancient civilizations, where trade was essential for survival. The Sumerians, around 3000 BC, are credited with developing the first form of writing, cuneiform, which they used to record business transactions.

Barter System: Initially, goods were exchanged directly through barter. This system had limitations, leading to the creation of money as a medium of exchange, facilitating easier and more efficient transactions.

Coinage: The Lydians, in what is now Turkey, were among the first to use coins as money in the 7th century BC. Coinage made trade simpler and more accessible.

Banking Origins: Ancient Rome saw the emergence of banking activities. Moneylenders would set up tables in the marketplaces, offering loans and exchanging currency.

Medieval Markets and Fairs: During the Middle Ages, local markets and periodic fairs were the centers of trade in Europe, where merchants from various regions would come to sell their goods.

Rise of the Merchant Class: The Renaissance period saw the rise of a wealthy and powerful merchant class, particularly in Italian city-states like Venice and Florence. This era also witnessed the emergence of double-entry bookkeeping, a significant advancement in business accounting introduced by Luca Pacioli in 1494.

Transformation of Production: The Industrial Revolution, starting in the late 18th century, transformed business practices with the introduction of mechanized production. This period saw a shift from artisanal, handcrafted goods to mass production in factories.

Expansion of Markets: Advances in transportation, like the steam engine and the railway, expanded markets and reduced the cost and time of shipping goods.

Corporations and Consumerism: The 20th century saw the rise of large corporations and the spread of consumer culture, facilitated by advances in marketing, branding, and mass media.

Globalization: The latter half of the 20th century was marked by the rapid globalization of business, driven by technological advancements in communication and transportation, leading to increasingly interconnected global markets.

Information Technology Revolution: The late 20th and early 21st centuries have been defined by the information technology revolution, fundamentally changing how businesses operate and compete.

E-Commerce and Social Media: The advent of the internet and the rise of social media platforms have transformed traditional business models, enabling global commerce and the rise of digital marketplaces.

From ancient trade routes to digital marketplaces, the history of business is a testament to human ingenuity and the relentless pursuit of growth and efficiency. As we look to the future, it's clear that technology will continue to play a pivotal role in shaping business practices, just as it has throughout history.

Chapter 1: The Chessboard - Understanding the Business Landscape

Concept: *Viewing the chessboard as the market landscape; understanding your position and the positions of your competitors.*

Standard 8x8 Wooden Chess Board

The chessboard is a simple 8x8 checkered board with alternating rows of black and white squares. In order to play the game of chess, you must understand a number of fundamentals, the pieces, the rules, but first you must look at the playing field. The board itself represents the battlefield – a space where strategic conflicts unfold, and victory is pursued with a combination of foresight, skill, and tactical acumen. The concept of business is the same way; before you play the game, you must understand the landscape and the playing field.

The business landscape is a complex arena where companies vie for dominance, armed with strategies aimed at outperforming competitors and capturing market share. Understanding this landscape is akin to mastering the intricacies of the chessboard, where every move counts, and every piece plays a crucial role in the overarching strategy.

The Setup: Assessing the Market

To set up the board of chess, you must ensure the chessboard is rotated in the correct orientation with the white squares diagonally descending from the top left of the board to the bottom right. The pieces also have specific squares to be placed, particularly the Queen being on her color in the center of the board.

Just as a chess player surveys the board before making the opening move, a business must first understand its market environment. This involves a deep dive into market research, competitor analysis, and customer insights. Recognizing the strengths and weaknesses of your competitors—be they knights and bishops or rival firms—enables you to position your company effectively.

Learn your playing field, get ready for the battlefield, and see your landscape. From there, understand your competitors, your position, their position, then set up accordingly.

Example: A tech startup entering the competitive landscape of social media apps must identify gaps left by popular giants like Facebook and Twitter. By understanding these platforms' limitations, the startup can tailor its product to offer unique features or cater to a niche audience, positioning itself as a rook or bishop that controls critical parts of the chessboard.

Controlling the Center: Market Positioning

In chess, controlling the center of the board is a well-established principle. It allows a player greater flexibility, more opportunities for attack, and better defense. In business, establishing a strong market position serves a similar purpose. It enables a company to leverage its strengths, respond more effectively to market changes, and shield itself from competitive threats.

For example, Amazon's foray into cloud computing with AWS wasn't just an expansion—it was a strategic move to control a central part of the digital economy's infrastructure. By offering scalable and affordable cloud services, Amazon positioned AWS as a dominant force, much like controlling the center of the chessboard.

Developing Your Pieces: Building Your Offerings

Development in chess involves moving your pieces into positions where they can exert their influence on the game. Every piece has a role, and their coordinated action creates a cohesive strategy. In business, this translates to developing your product lines, services, and operational capabilities in a way that supports your overall strategy and market positioning.

Example: Apple's development of the iPhone was not merely about launching a new product; it was about placing a piece on the business chessboard that would extend its influence across multiple segments—telecommunications, music, photography, and mobile computing. The iPhone became a queen on Apple's board, a powerful asset around which other strategies were constructed.

Anticipating Moves: Market Forecasting

A skilled chess player doesn't just react to an opponent's moves; they anticipate them, planning several moves ahead. Similarly, successful businesses forecast market trends, competitor actions, and technological advancements to shape their strategies proactively.

Example: Netflix's shift from DVD rentals to streaming services was a strategic anticipation of changing consumer preferences and technological trends. By foreseeing the move towards online content consumption, Netflix positioned itself ahead of traditional media companies, securing a dominant position in the streaming landscape.

Understanding the business landscape requires the same strategic depth and foresight as mastering the chessboard. By analyzing the market, positioning your company effectively, developing your offerings strategically, and anticipating future moves, you can navigate the complexities of the business world with the skill of a chess grandmaster. The lessons from the chessboard are clear: success, whether in chess or in business, begins with a deep understanding of the terrain upon which the game is played.

As we progress through this book, we'll continue to draw parallels between chess strategies and business tactics, uncovering insights that can guide your journey in the competitive world of business.

Chapter 2: Pawns - The Value of Every Team Member

Concept: *Each pawn on the chessboard can play a critical role, similar to every employee in a company.*

In the game of chess, pawns may seem like the least powerful pieces on the board, but their strategic importance cannot be understated. They form the game's backbone, protecting more valuable pieces, controlling key squares, and possessing the unique ability to transform into any piece if they reach the opposite side of the board. This chapter draws parallels between the role of pawns in chess and the value of every team member in a business setting, emphasizing the significance of empowering all employees, regardless of their position.

The Unsung Heroes

Much like pawns, individual contributors in a business often do not receive the limelight that senior executives or star performers do. However, their contributions are critical to the organization's overall success. Each team member, from the front-line customer service representative to the back-office staff, plays a unique role that supports the larger business strategy.

Furthermore, in the game of chess, it is a common strategy for players to sacrifice the pawns in order to gain better positioning known as tactical advantage. Whilst this is not to encouraging sacrificing team members, a similar understanding can be said to utilizing pawns and team members for certain positions or delegation in order to strategize a winning position from other positions.

Example: Consider a tech company where software engineers are seen as the driving force. While their work is undoubtedly crucial, the efforts of the sales team to understand and communicate customer needs, the marketing team's strategies to position the product effectively, and the customer support team's role in retaining clients are all equally important for sustained success.

Strategic Positioning

In chess, the strategic positioning of pawns can control the game's flow, creating opportunities for attack and defense. Similarly, in business, placing the right people in positions where they can use their strengths to the fullest can create significant competitive advantages.

Example: A retail business may thrive not just because of its product selection but because of the strategic positioning of its customer service staff. Well-trained, empathetic customer service personnel, positioned at critical points in the customer journey, can turn potential complaints into positive experiences, enhancing brand loyalty.

Potential for Transformation

The pawn's ability to promote to a more powerful piece upon reaching the far side of the board is a metaphor for the growth and development potential within each employee. Encouraging continuous learning and providing opportunities for advancement can transform an entry-level employee into a future leader.

Example: A small startup may have limited roles initially, but as it grows, opportunities for team members to lead projects, manage teams, or spearhead new initiatives emerge. Those who began as "pawns" in the company can become "queens," driving the business forward with their vision and leadership.

The Collective Force

A group of pawns working together in chess can form a formidable structure, protecting each other and controlling significant portions of the board. In business, fostering teamwork and collaboration among all levels of employees can lead to a strong, united front capable of overcoming challenges and achieving collective goals.

Example: In project management, the collective efforts of the project team, each member contributing their expertise and supporting one another, can lead to the successful completion of complex projects, on time and within budget.

The lesson from the chessboard is clear: do not underestimate the value of the pawns, the individual team members who, day in and day out, contribute to your business's success. By recognizing their importance, strategically positioning them to use their strengths, and fostering their growth and development, you can create a resilient, adaptable organization poised for long-term success. Just as in chess, where pawns can turn the tide of the game, in business, every team member holds potential power to influence outcomes positively.

Chapter 3: Rooks, Knights, and Bishops - Leveraging Your Assets

Concept: *Utilizing your business assets (rooks, knights, bishops) strategically for maximum impact.*

In the grand strategy of chess, rooks, knights, and bishops play distinctive roles, each with their unique abilities to maneuver and influence the board. These pieces are pivotal in orchestrating both defense and attack, their value magnified by strategic deployment and synergy. Drawing a parallel to the business world, this chapter delves into leveraging a company's assets—its people, products, and processes—to carve a competitive edge and drive success.

Rooks: The Pillars of Strength

In chess, rooks are powerful pieces, moving across the board in straight lines. They symbolize the foundational assets of a business, such as robust infrastructure, capital, and technology. These assets provide the framework upon which businesses build their operations and strategies.

Example: A logistics company's fleet of vehicles (its "rooks") enables it to offer fast and reliable delivery services, a cornerstone of its value proposition. Investing in state-of-the-art logistics technology enhances these assets, allowing for efficient route planning and real-time tracking, thereby reinforcing the company's market position.

Knights: Agility and Innovation

Knights move in a unique L-shaped pattern, capable of jumping over other pieces, embodying agility and unpredictability. In business, these qualities are mirrored in a company's ability to innovate and adapt swiftly to changing market conditions.

Example: A tech startup, much like a knight, capitalizes on its agility to disrupt traditional markets with innovative solutions. By pivoting quickly based on customer feedback and emerging trends, the startup outmaneuvers larger, more established companies, capturing market share and driving growth.

Bishops: Diagonal Vision

Bishops move diagonally, covering long distances across the board, representing a business's ability to identify and leverage market trends and opportunities that are not immediately obvious. This strategic vision, akin to a bishop's long-range influence, allows businesses to position themselves advantageously within their industry.

Example: A renewable energy company, seeing the diagonal "lines" of societal shifts toward sustainability, invests early in solar and wind technology. This foresight positions the company as a leader in the renewable sector, tapping into growing consumer demand for clean energy.

<u>Leveraging Synergy</u>

The combined use of rooks, knights, and bishops in chess demonstrates the power of leveraging diverse assets for a cohesive strategy. Similarly, businesses thrive by integrating their various assets—infrastructure, innovation, and strategic vision—into a unified approach that aligns with their goals and market demands.

Example: An e-commerce platform integrates its robust IT infrastructure ("rooks") with an innovative customer service approach ("knights") and a strategic understanding of consumer behavior ("bishops"). This synergy creates a seamless shopping experience, driving customer satisfaction and loyalty.

Understanding and leveraging your business assets—your "rooks," "knights," and "bishops"—are crucial for crafting strategies that lead to sustainable success. By recognizing the unique value and potential of each asset, aligning them with your strategic objectives, and fostering their interplay, you can outmaneuver competitors and secure a winning position in the market. Just as in chess, the strategic deployment and coordination of these assets are key to capturing the king—achieving your business goals.

Chapter 4: The Queen - Maximizing Your Key Players

Concept: The queen is your most versatile and powerful piece, akin to your key resources or personnel in business.

The queen, with her unparalleled versatility and power on the chessboard, serves as a pivotal force in the game of chess. Her ability to move in any direction—horizontally, vertically, or diagonally—and cover vast distances in a single move makes her the most valuable piece. In the realm of business, the queen symbolizes your key players or core competencies—those critical elements, whether people, products, or services, that drive your business forward and differentiate you in the marketplace.

Identifying Your Queens

The first step in leveraging this powerful asset is identifying who or what your "queens" are. In a company, this could be a top-performing salesperson, a proprietary technology, or a unique service offering. These key players have the potential to make significant impacts, drive innovation, and capture market share.

Example: In a technology firm, a patented software algorithm that significantly enhances data processing speed may be considered the company's queen. Its unique capability offers a competitive edge, attracting clients and setting the firm apart from competitors.

Positioning for Maximum Impact

Just as the strategic placement of the queen on a chessboard can dictate the flow of the game, positioning your key players in roles or markets where they can make the most significant impact is crucial. This involves aligning their strengths with the company's strategic objectives and ensuring they have the resources and support to excel.

Example: A multinational corporation identifies its customer service excellence as its queen. By positioning this strength at the forefront of its brand identity and investing in training and technology to enhance customer interactions, the company strengthens its reputation and builds customer loyalty.

Protecting Your Queens

In chess, losing the queen can be a devastating blow that often leads to defeat. Similarly, in business, it's essential to protect your key assets. This means safeguarding proprietary technologies with patents, retaining top talent with competitive compensation and a positive work culture, and continuously innovating to stay ahead of the competition.

Example: A biotech company with a groundbreaking drug invests in rigorous patent protection and research and development to create next-generation treatments, ensuring its market leadership and protecting its queen from competitors.

Leveraging Synergy

While the queen is the most powerful piece, her effectiveness is maximized when working in concert with other pieces. In business, this translates to creating synergies between your key players and other assets or departments within the company. Collaboration and integration can amplify your competitive advantage, leading to greater innovation and success.

Example: An e-commerce giant leverages its logistics network (its rooks) and data analytics capabilities (its bishops) to support its core competency in customer experience (its queen), creating a seamless and personalized shopping journey that drives sales and customer loyalty.

The queen in chess teaches us the importance of recognizing, positioning, and protecting our key players in business. By maximizing the impact of your core competencies, safeguarding them against threats, and fostering synergy with other assets, you can navigate the competitive landscape with the confidence and strategic acumen of a seasoned chess player. Remember, while the queen is a game-changer, her power is most potent when used as part of a broader, cohesive strategy.

Chapter 5: The King - Protecting Your Core

Concept: The objective of chess is to protect the king, similar to safeguarding your business's core mission and values.

In the intricate game of chess, the king is the most crucial piece. Although not as agile or powerful as some other pieces, its safety determines the game's outcome. Analogously, in the business world, your core business—your company's essential mission, values, and key assets—needs to be vigilantly protected. This chapter delves into strategies for safeguarding your core business against threats and ensuring its longevity and stability.

Identifying Your Core

Before you can protect your king, you must identify what constitutes your "king" in the business context. This could be your unique value proposition, proprietary technology, key customer base, or even your brand reputation. Understanding what is at the heart of your business is the first step in devising strategies to protect it.

Example: A cloud computing company might consider its data centers and the technology infrastructure that enables high-speed, secure data processing as its core. Protecting this involves not just physical security measures but also safeguarding intellectual property and ensuring robust cybersecurity.

Fortifying Your Position

In chess, the positioning of pieces around the king is strategic, designed to fortify defenses while maintaining flexibility. Similarly, businesses must build strong defenses around their core, which might involve legal protections such as patents and trademarks, strategic partnerships that provide mutual support, and developing a loyal customer base that can act as a buffer against competitive threats.

Example: A pharmaceutical company relies on patents to protect its core products, but it also invests in research and development to ensure a pipeline of new drugs that can sustain the business once older patents expire.

Monitoring Threats

Awareness of potential threats is crucial in chess, as it is in business. Constantly monitoring the competitive landscape, regulatory changes, technological advancements, and market trends can help you anticipate and prepare for challenges to your core business.

Example: An e-commerce platform keeps a close watch on emerging technologies that could change consumer shopping habits, such as augmented reality, and explores ways to integrate these into their offering to stay ahead of potential disruptors.

Adapting to Challenges

Protecting your king in chess often requires adapting your strategy in response to your opponent's moves. In business, this means being prepared to pivot your strategies, innovate your offerings, or even redefine your core business in response to changing market dynamics.

Example: A traditional publishing house, recognizing the shift towards digital media, might protect its core mission of storytelling by transitioning into e-books and audiobooks, thus adapting to the digital age while safeguarding its foundational purpose.

The Importance of Resilience

Finally, the resilience of the king in chess lies not in its ability to strike back but in its capacity to endure. Building resilience into your business model—through diversification, financial prudence, and fostering a strong organizational culture—ensures that your core business can withstand adversities.

Example: A family-owned restaurant chain, facing the challenge of pandemic-related closures, pivots to offering takeout and delivery services, demonstrating resilience by adapting its business model to continue serving its customer base.

Protecting your core business in a rapidly changing and competitive environment requires a multifaceted approach: identifying what needs to be protected, fortifying your defenses, staying vigilant against threats, adapting with agility, and building resilience. By embodying the strategic depth of protecting the king in chess, you can ensure the longevity and success of your business in the face of any challenge.

Chapter 6: Check and Checkmate - Competitive Strategies

Concept: *Understanding offensive and defensive strategies in chess and how they can be applied to overcome business challenges and outmaneuver competitors.*

The climax of a chess game lies in delivering a checkmate, a move that captures the opponent's king with no escape. This decisive moment requires foresight, precision, and an understanding of one's own strengths and the opponent's vulnerabilities. In the business world, achieving a metaphorical checkmate means executing competitive strategies that secure market leadership and ensure long-term success. This chapter explores how to outmaneuver competitors and position your business for victory.

Understanding the Competitive Landscape

Just as a chess player surveys the board to assess threats and opportunities, businesses must thoroughly understand their competitive landscape. This involves analyzing competitors' strengths, weaknesses, strategies, and potential moves.

Example: A beverage company might conduct a SWOT analysis to understand its position relative to major competitors in the market, identifying opportunities for differentiation in product offerings or marketing strategies.

Exploiting Opportunities

In chess, exploiting a gap in your opponent's defense can lead to victory. Similarly, businesses can achieve success by identifying and capitalizing on market opportunities that competitors have overlooked or are unable to address effectively.

Example: Spotting a rising trend in consumer preference for plant-based products, a food company quickly diversifies its product line to include vegan options, capturing a significant share of this growing market before its competitors.

Defensive Strategies

Defense is as crucial as offense in chess, protecting your king while planning your next move. In business, defensive strategies might involve safeguarding your market share, protecting intellectual property, or maintaining customer loyalty against competitive threats.

Example: A tech company facing new entrants in its market might invest in customer loyalty programs and enhance its product ecosystem to make it more difficult for customers to switch to competitors.

The Endgame: Strategic Moves Towards Victory

As a chess match approaches the endgame, each move becomes critical. Businesses, too, must make strategic decisions that will secure their market position and ensure long-term profitability.

Example: A retailer facing stiff competition may decide to focus on e-commerce, leveraging analytics to offer personalized shopping experiences, thereby gaining an edge over competitors who are slow to adopt digital strategies.

Learning from Defeat

In both chess and business, not every battle will end in victory. Learning from defeats is crucial for growth. Analyzing what went wrong, adjusting strategies, and coming back stronger is key to eventual success.

Example: After losing significant market share to a competitor with a more innovative product, a company revisits its R&D strategy to foster a culture of innovation, ensuring it stays competitive in future market dynamics.

Achieving a checkmate in the business world requires a combination of understanding the competitive landscape, exploiting opportunities, employing defensive strategies, and making strategic moves that align with the company's long-term goals. Just like in chess, the path to victory involves strategic planning, adaptability, and the wisdom to learn from both victories and defeats. By applying these principles, businesses can navigate the complexities of the competitive market and emerge victorious, securing their position as leaders in their industry.

Chapter 7: Endgame Strategies - Planning for the Long Term

Concept: *Importance of endgame strategies in chess and their parallels in business succession planning, exit strategies, and long-term vision.*

The endgame in chess is about meticulously maneuvering limited pieces to secure a win. It requires foresight, precision, and a clear understanding of your ultimate goal. Similarly, in business, the endgame involves long-term planning and execution strategies that ensure sustainable success and legacy. This chapter explores how businesses can effectively navigate their endgame, focusing on future growth, succession planning, and adapting to changing market landscapes.

Vision and Goal Setting

Just as a chess player envisions their path to checkmate, businesses must have a clear vision of what they aim to achieve in the long term. This involves setting specific, measurable, ambitious, relevant, and time-bound (SMART) goals that guide the direction and growth of the company.

Example: A renewable energy startup sets a 20-year goal to power one million homes using sustainable energy sources. This vision guides its research, funding, and expansion strategies, focusing efforts on achieving significant impact and growth.

Succession Planning

In chess, each move is made with consideration for the next several moves. In business, this translates to succession planning—preparing for the future leadership of the company to ensure continuity and stability. This involves identifying potential leaders early and investing in their development.

Example: A family-owned manufacturing company begins leadership training for the next generation years in advance, involving them in strategic decisions and gradually increasing their responsibilities to ensure a smooth transition when the time comes.

Adapting to Change

The endgame in chess often requires adapting strategies based on the evolving state of the board. Similarly, businesses must remain adaptable, ready to pivot their strategies in response to technological advancements, market trends, and consumer behaviors.

Example: A bookstore chain, seeing the rise of digital e-books, diversifies its business model to include online sales, e-book subscriptions, and community events, thus adapting to the changing landscape while staying true to its core mission of fostering a love for reading.

Building a Legacy

Ultimately, the endgame is about more than just winning; it's about leaving a lasting impact. Businesses should aim to build a legacy that transcends immediate profits, focusing on contributing positively to their industry, community, and the broader society.

Example: A technology firm not only innovates within its sector but also commits to ethical practices, supports STEM education initiatives, and implements environmentally friendly operations, aiming to leave a positive mark on the world.

Navigating the endgame in business requires long-term vision, careful planning, adaptability, and a commitment to building a legacy. By applying endgame strategies from chess, leaders can guide their companies toward not just immediate victories but sustained success and a lasting impact. The endgame reminds us that while tactical wins are important, the ultimate goal is to achieve a position of enduring strength and value.

Chapter 8: Advanced Strategies in Chess and Business

In both chess and business, mastering the fundamentals is only the beginning. True excellence requires delving into advanced strategies that leverage deep insights, innovative thinking, and strategic foresight. This chapter explores sophisticated approaches in chess that have direct parallels in the art of business management and development, offering guidance on navigating complex competitive landscapes with precision and creativity.

Leveraging Opponent's Weaknesses

In chess, grandmasters excel not only by playing to their strengths but also by exploiting their opponents' vulnerabilities. Similarly, successful businesses conduct thorough competitor analysis to identify weaknesses in the market that can be leveraged to gain a competitive edge.

Sometimes winning doesn't come from outplaying your opponent so thoroughly, but simply from being stable until your opponent exhibits weaknesses, mistakes, or blunders. In chess, the top grandmasters sometimes say they simply win because luck is on their side on some days. The same is true for business. The opponents cannot be controlled, so ensuring your position is firm can help create luck.

Example: A software company might notice that its main competitor's product lacks certain features desired by the market. By developing these features in their own product, the company can capture a larger market share, effectively turning their opponent's weakness into their own strategic advantage.

Sacrifice for Greater Gain

A common advanced strategy in chess is the tactical sacrifice of a piece to gain a more favorable position or lead to a checkmate. In business, this can translate to short-term sacrifices for long-term gains, such as investing heavily in research and development or temporarily lowering prices to enter a new market.

Example: An automotive company might sacrifice short-term profits by investing in electric vehicle technology. While this may initially reduce their financial margins, it positions them as leaders in a growing market segment, ensuring long-term sustainability and profitability.

Positional Play and Strategic Patience

Advanced chess players often engage in positional play, making subtle moves that improve their position without immediate material gain. In business, this equates to strategies that may not yield immediate results but strategically position the company for future success.

Example: A retail company might invest in creating an exceptional customer experience, from store design to staff training, without directly pushing sales. This strategic patience fosters brand loyalty and customer satisfaction, driving long-term revenue growth.

Forking, Pinning, En Passant and Discovery

In the game of chess, sometimes some moves hold more than just their face-value move. The tactic of forking two pieces or more allows, or pinning a piece to another can sometimes create tactics and surprises that the opponent underestimates or misses completely. These strategies can be utilized in business in the same way.

Example: A tech giant focuses on dominating the cloud computing sector, recognizing its strategic importance in the digital economy. By offering innovative, scalable solutions, the company establishes itself as an indispensable service provider, securing a dominant market position.

Advanced strategies in chess and business require a deep understanding of the game, an ability to think several moves ahead, and the creativity to devise and execute plans that outmaneuver opponents. By studying and applying these advanced concepts, business leaders can navigate the complexities of their industries with the skill and finesse of a chess grandmaster, turning strategic insights into tangible success.

As we reach the conclusion of "Think Chess - Win Business," it's clear that the realms of chess and business, seemingly disparate at first glance, are intricately connected by the threads of strategy, decision-making, and competitive dynamics. This book has taken you on a journey through the nuanced parallels between the ancient game of chess and the modern world of business, revealing that the principles guiding successful players on the chessboard can also lead to triumph in the boardroom.

We began by understanding the chessboard itself, a metaphor for the business landscape, where positioning and foresight set the stage for success. We explored the significance of each chess piece, from the humble pawn to the powerful queen, drawing lessons on the value of every team member, the importance of key players, and the strategic utilization of resources. The roles of knights, bishops, and rooks were examined, emphasizing agility, vision, and strength—qualities equally vital in navigating the complexities of the business world.

The concept of "Check and Checkmate" highlighted the culmination of strategic efforts in both chess and business, teaching us the importance of recognizing opportunities, executing decisive moves, and understanding the competition. We delved into the art of defense and the necessity of protecting our core assets, akin to safeguarding the king on the chessboard. The discussion on endgame strategies reminded us that success is not just about the immediate wins but also about planning for sustainable growth and legacy.

"Think Chess - Win Business" has underscored the power of strategic thinking, the value of anticipating your opponent's moves, and the importance of adaptability and resilience. It has shown that, just as in chess, business leaders must be adept at reading the game, understanding their position, and making calculated decisions that leverage their strengths and exploit the weaknesses of the competition.

In closing, let this book serve as a guide to thinking like a chess master in your business endeavors. Embrace the strategic mindset, the patience, and the creativity that chess demands. Apply these lessons to your business strategies, and you will navigate the challenges and opportunities of the business world with greater skill and confidence. The path to victory, both on the chessboard and in business, is paved with the insights, tactics, and philosophies explored in these pages. May you move forward with the wisdom of a grandmaster, ready to make your next move your best move.

www.ingramcontent.com/pod-product-compliance
Lightning Source LLC
Chambersburg PA
CBHW071444210326
41597CB00020B/3936